SECRET MILLIONAIRE

how to be a millionaire

Copyright © 2019 by secret millionaire

All rights reserved. No part of this publication may be reproduced, stored or transmitted in any form or by any means, electronic, mechanical, photocopying, recording, scanning, or otherwise without written permission from the publisher. It is illegal to copy this book, post it to a website, or distribute it by any other means without permission.

First edition

This book was professionally typeset on Reedsy. Find out more at reedsy.com

Contents

Millionaire Mindset – Habits	v
Implement the word now	1
Hour of power	3
Stubbornness	5
Meditation	7
Healthy Breakfast	8
Put myself in first place	10
Get your head right	12
Sports on the morning	14
Sleep early and get up early	16
Reading Books	18
Lunch Break	20
day's structure	22
Journal of happiness	24
Wealth planning meeting	26
Significant decision	28
Uncomfortable actions	30
Proper Use of Our Body	32
Limit Screen Time	34
Bank account	36
Positive balance	38
Saving	40
Make Money a Love	42
Ask why	44

Work with your strengths	46
Strongest strength	48
Get advice	50
Talk about your dream	52
Writing Your Dream	54
Think big and set big goals	56
Mirror	58
Help with the money	60
Secretly giving	62
Gratitude	64
Bless	66
The End	68

Millionaire Mindset - Habits

The first thing to becoming a millionaire its to develop habits of millionaire.
So without unnecessary words let's dive in and make your life rich and happy.

1

Implement the word now

Implement the word **now** - everything is happening now. It is more important to make a decision now than the right one. One should not be afraid of making the wrong decision because it can only be learned from it. What's more, we can never know if the decision is true. There has to be an obsession with decision making now and that's what will change life end to end. Self-confidence is the result of quick decision making.

Those who take time in decision-making show less confidence in themselves.

2

Hour of power

Choose an hour a day and it will be your hour of power - this is an hour when you self-concept that you are a multi-millionaire. At this hour you can learn something new and enriching, read biographies of rich people. It doesn't have to be a continuous hour, it can be divided during the day. At this time you read books, meditate, exercise, watch content and other things that give you a sense of empowerment.

HOW TO BE A MILLIONAIRE

your hour of power

3

Stubbornness

Stubbornness to stick to our path and rituals - even when you step away, you always have to return to the new path you have built for yourself. The highest level of commitment must be assimilated to the change we have chosen. Background noise from the environment and ourselves should be ignored and always back on track. There must be total business success. And to do that you have to be at 100% energy all the time. Always maintain maximum alertness and be fully focused on any business, home, or interpersonal action.

HOW TO BE A MILLIONAIRE

you have to be at 100% energy all the time

4

Meditation

Meditation Practice - Meditation is a tool for balancing and connecting the mind and body.

connect to your soul

5

Healthy Breakfast

Healthy Breakfast - Sit in the morning and do nothing but eat breakfast. The first stop of the day has to be made already this morning. This is an important stage that must not be missed. It also cleanses and purifies in terms of consciousness, to start the day "clear". It is advisable to cook your own breakfast. What matters most is making this stop and dedicating this time to yourself (even at the cost of getting up earlier to make time for it). Eat natural things that enrich you such as vegetables, fruits and high protein foods. It is important to open the morning in health, or in food

A nutrient that gives the body energy.

HEALTHY BREAKFAST

Healthy Breakfast

6

Put myself in first place

Put myself in first place already in the morning - think how I would like my morning to look. What is my favorite activity to do first thing in the morning. Not thinking what doesn't or what most concerns us (home or work subjects). You have to write what is your perfect morning and how I would like it to look.

perfect morning

7

Get your head right

Get your head right - the key to arranging the head is first to arrange my environment. Desktop, office, home, etc. Whenever there is a flood, our environment needs to be tidied up. Take a few minutes to arrange our stuff so things are sorted out. Self-arranging actions in the subconscious create order in mind. The brain sends a broadcast and then as they sit on the issues of our business then the brain thinks in a more organized and mature way. You hve millionare that washing dishes at home once a day and does that because it's no importance but beacuse it's clean the head and makes room for maximum creativity. You need to spend 15-10 minutes a day doing something that is not so important to clear your head. It can be anything that clears your mind.

Maximum creativity

8

Sports on the morning

Sports on the morning - open the morning with exercise. Even just fifteen minutes walk. It's not good to start your morning with too much exercise, enough short 15-minute activity with a high-level pulse - not too much. It is critical for creative thinking, organizing, and oxygen flow to the body. For those who are having difficulty: make socks and shoes by the bed and imagine how we do this activity in the morning.

Sports on the morning

9

Sleep early and get up early

Sleep early and get up early - The ideal is to sleep for 8 hours when going to bed at 10:00 pm and wake up at 6 am. That's how you start your day at Clear which contributes to productivity and allows plenty of time until late morning. That means having to plan your dreams as early in the morning and not just at night. Night people are frameless people so they do not have a set hour and must set an hour when they go to bed and an hour when they get up. It is healthy and necessary to get rich and direct ourselves to the frame of sleep and the brain is wiring itself to the rest time needed.

SLEEP EARLY AND GET UP EARLY

Dream in the morning

10

Reading Books

Reading Books - Reading books is critical to success. Something needs to be done for reading and summarizing the books. Jay Abraham said: "For rich people big libraries, for poor people big TVs." It is advisable to read on the one hand training and psychology books, infant books, mindset books and on the other hand biography books, strategic books, personal stories of people, interviews with people. Reading these books is akin to sowing seeds. Along with the habits and rituals, it is the watering of the seeds and it will allow the creation of a new businessman. And it's important to understand that not everyone fits. The same habit of reading. You have to find the right time to read depending on the type of person we are. If the book lulls us, that's a positive thing. If a book wakes us up then you have to read in the morning. It is important to read these books slowly and deeply in order to think about and delve into them.

"For rich people big libraries, for poor people big TVs."

11

Lunch Break

Lunch Break - Once a day, in the middle of the day, take a full hour break when you are not talking about work. At lunch, have lunch, rest and talk about your life. Don't waste your time on social networks. Invest time in relationships, in the people around you, call close people and engage in life.

LUNCH BREAK

Lunch Break

12

day's structure

A day's structure with clear roof times - The day's structure should be with a fixed start time, a break in the middle, and a fixed time at which one finishes. It is most effective to end a day at 6:00 pm. Once you set your mindset to an end time, then you can do the most because they become more concentrated within the time frame. And you have to remember there is always tomorrow. One should not reach a state of exhaustion or power Bode at the expense of personal life. There is always tomorrow and the day can be arranged differently. It is important to introduce ourselves to the hourly defined framework.

Day's structure

13

Journal of happiness

Keep a journal of happiness - In the evening, when you are free, you have to put in one thing every day that defines us and makes us feel happy. It has to be put in the journal. Once it's in front of our eyes it creates a passion and makes us happier. In summary, one thing every day needs to be done that makes us happy (even if it only takes one minute) and put it in a journal.

Journal of happiness

14

Wealth planning meeting

Open the day at a wealth planning meeting - before starting our work day, spend between 20 minutes and an hour answering the question: What is the one significant thing I'm going to do today to get rich in the future? And what next are two or three significant things I'm going to do today to get rich in the future? It should be a regular habit. This meeting may have been done with a partner, colleague or staff. You have to think and talk big, in the millions. You have to speak, think and plan in this language - big time. It will help the brain open up for things to come by themselves.

WEALTH PLANNING MEETING

wealth planning meeting

15

Significant decision

Make one significant decision a day - ask ourselves at the beginning or end of the day what significant decision I make about this day. Put this in the power hour list. You have to sit down and make one significant decision one day. Once you start doing this regularly the brain and the subconscious will get used to making big decisions.

Significant decision

16

Uncomfortable actions

Do two uncomfortable actions until 11 am - the further the previous habit, the more meaningful and large the decision is the less convenient. So you have to do two things that aren't used to doing until 11:00. Do things we don't like to deal with, small, quick things that don't take time - until 11:00. It allows you to start the momentum from the comfort zone. Richard Branson says: "You have to be at ease to do what's uncomfortable." So we feel comfortable. To do uncomfortable chores.

UNCOMFORTABLE ACTIONS

Uncomfortable actions

17

Proper Use of Our Body

Proper Use of Our Body - This is an energy-boosting technique. During the day the body gets used to comfort in this area. Effectiveness, productivity and creativity begin to decline. Therefore, one time per hour is required to make physiological changes. That is to do a short exercise every hour, preferably with your team, to bring back productivity.

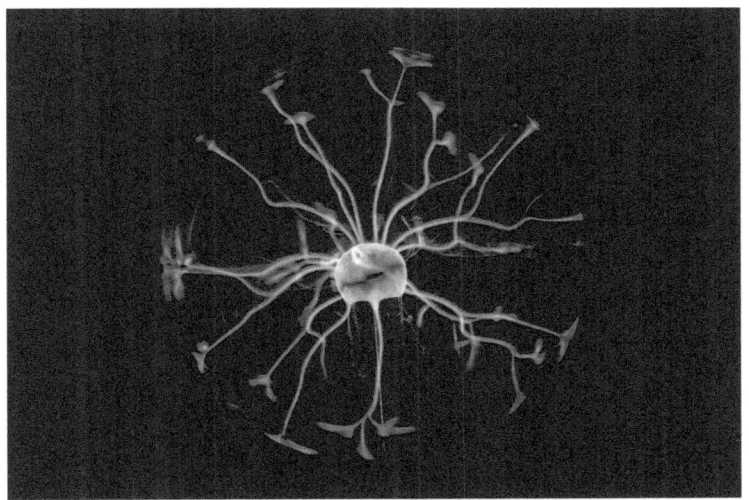

Energy-Boosting technique

18

Limit Screen Time

Limit Screen Time - Limit time in front of our laptop, or in front of the computer if it saves us time other than working time. It has to be put into a frame (such as the dancer). Social networking should be done when and when not. In the hour before going to sleep - disconnect from social networks to save ourselves quality time reading, watching rich content, etc. and not social networks that will hurt quality sleep before bedtime.

LIMIT SCREEN TIME

Limit Screen Time

19

Bank account

Login your bank account once a day - even if there is almost no traffic in the current account, you still need to check your bank account on a day-to-day basis - this is a habit of management. In order to identify "surprises" that we should not have been charged for, in addition to managing cash flow that will also show us what is going to happen and not just what has already happened. Need a flow for the home and family economy and a separate cash flow for the business.

BANK ACCOUNT

Bank account

20

Positive balance

Getting used to being in positive balance- It has an important energetic element of consciousness. It is better to take out loans than a minus rate on a bank account (even if it costs more in interest). The business attitude is always to see that you are in the plus (positive balance), and you have to get used to the fact that the positive balance is constantly growing. This is how the brain is used to always being a positive balance and completely forgetting about minus and dislike it.

Positive balance

21

Saving

Take care of saving every day - Adopt a habit of saving money. People who save work for their savings and get used to saving money. It is advisable to make a loan at a new bank - without quick access or credit card - and to return a fixed amount of direct deposit for a certain amount of savings. In addition, make savings for children so that at the age of 18 they will have the amount of money to do whatever they decide.

SAVING

Saving every day

22

Make Money a Love

Make Money a Love - Start fiddling with money and stop being afraid of it. Engage it from a positive rather than a negative place like most of the population. To do this, the energy of money must be turned into positive energy. So you have to embrace a generous habit - get used to being generous with money and find ways to be generous with it (donate, etc.). Don't just spend and get into debt but pay off with your money (if I bought myself then on the way to buy for others too). Be generous with the money and it will be appreciated and it will allow the energy of the money to work better than the smallest thing

The biggest talk.

Love money

23

Ask why

Ask why? - The most powerful thing that reveals your mission. This is why you do what you do.

Ask why? – The most powerful tool you have

24

Work with your strengths

Only work with your strengths - not improve weaknesses, etc., work only with your strengths. Give someone else to deal with what we're less good at. Strengthening weaknesses is staying with weaknesses versus strengthening strengths that will lift us more up. We need to make a list of your strengths - the things we love and love ourselves, that we would like to pass on to our child or our employees too - and think about what will strengthen our strengths. What actions should be taken to enhance our strengths. It is also advisable to consult people on how to improve our strengths.

WORK WITH YOUR STRENGTHS

Work with your strengths

25

Strongest strength

Do each day with your strongest strength – once a day to do youstrongeststrength . Which gives the most energy and motivation. Find the way to do it every day.

STRONGEST STRENGTH

It's like a tree at first as you water it and give it nutrients it will grow to be a strong tree with strong roots

26

Get advice

Get advice from someone who's already done it - pay attention to who I pay attention to. You have to pay attention to who I take my advice from and just take advice from the person who applies things himself and not just talk about it. The best coaches are the players themselves. Need to learn from business people in our field. Check out and learn how successful entrepreneurs - in our field and in general - have done it.

GET ADVICE

Successful entrepreneurs

27

Talk about your dream

Talk about your dream - **YOU** Must talk about yours dream, even if it is just something mysterious about change. Once set A high-level dream sees rapid progress toward the target. Have to dream Big and then wonders are created. You have to say the dream over and over and over again in grandiose terms in order to increase his chances of succeeding and coming true.

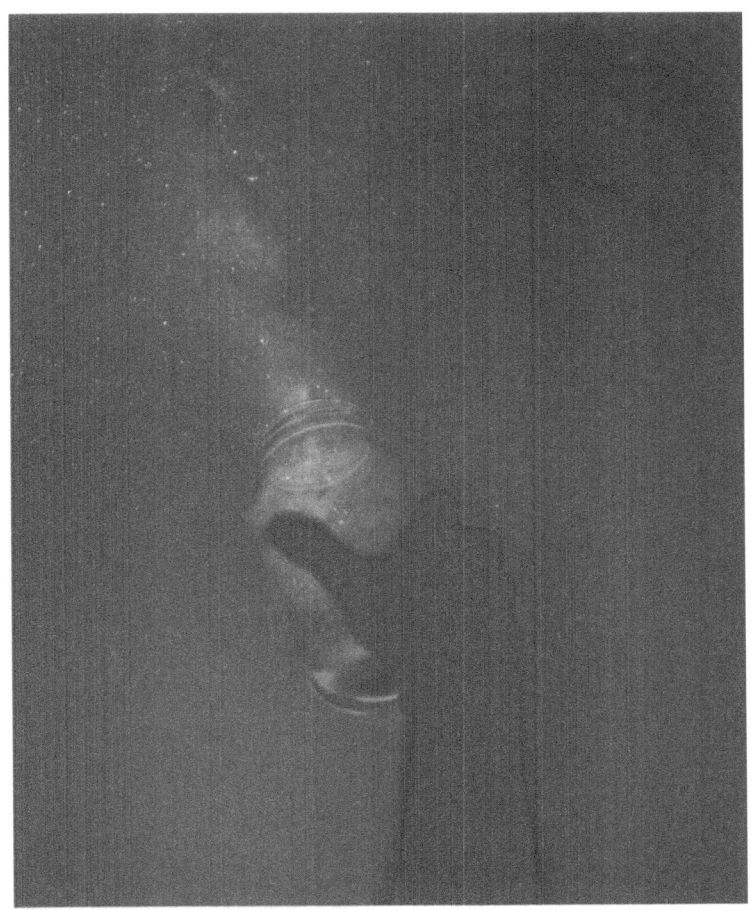

Dream Big

28

Writing Your Dream

Writing Your Dream - Writing has added value in life. It creates reality. Throughout history when people wrote future-oriented things - they created the future. We need to write our dream one year ahead. And every time you have to go back to it and upgrade and improve it to create our future. Because what writing is happening. You have to write the future (day / week / month / year) in a one-page frame.

WRITING YOUR DREAM

Writing Your Dream

29

Think big and set big goals

Think big and set big goals - everything we do should be considered a big and meaningful thing and give it the big meaning it needs to have. It creates a commitment and caring towards the same thing which has given supreme significance. Do everything in the best possible way. Even if it is self-persuasion - it will give you the motivation and understanding that everything is important and everything is important.

Think big and set big goals

30

Mirror

Saying in front of the mirror what I'm going to do - Whenever you come across a mirror you have to stop, look into your eyes and say what we're going to do at the greatest possible level and what our dream is. Saying words in front of the mirror what we are going to do and why we are going to do it and what it means. Every encounter with this sight is an opportunity to talk to the subconscious and it should be a habit that changes and adds to the fun of life.

MIRROR

Look into your eyes

31

Help with the money

To whom are you going to help with the money - find who we are going to help with our money. Who can we donate to, even if it is a small amount every month? Look into the eyes of who we are donating to really deal with who we help with the money. Finding regularly to give and donate as part of our schedule and as a habit for anything and everything. It's a life-changing habit.

HELP WITH THE MONEY

Help

32

Secretly giving

Secretly giving - finding someone or something that contributes to it in secret. It is an important habit for the energy of money and it is important that this donation is made in secret. This is a wonderful and important thing to use and most importantly keep it secret.

Secretly giving

33

Gratitude

Gratitude - Appreciation. Every day I write (morning or night) 20 things I appreciate. It causes the brain to be phenomenally programmed. It changes our frequency. In the near future, write thank you for things related to our success, growth, money or wealth. Write the link to thank you: about the business, the career, etc. Write things about money and our revenue. As soon as the magnets are honored, there are other things. Focus on success, income, passion and a successful career. That should be the focus.

Gratitude

34

Bless

Bless- welcome the positive, negative, material and human things: people, workers, money, desk, computer, etc. Constantly blessing others and receiving or subtracting. Bless every blessing that comes out of your mouth and changes the energy we have. Blessing is the recognition of goodness and it will radiate on us. We need to put the focus of blessings on business success and so the blessing will come back to us.

BLESS

Bless

The End

You have just received the 34 habits of rich and happy people and not just the rich.
Every day you will add one thing to your habits and within a month and a half from now you will experience change and empowerment in your life that will be expressed in both happiness and wealth for you and for your family.
Within six months of reading the book and applying brain habits.
Yours and your subconscious will create a rich and fulfilling life for you.

Enjoy the journey to creating wealth and happiness.

www.ingramcontent.com/pod-product-compliance
Lightning Source LLC
Chambersburg PA
CBHW020611220526
45463CB00006B/2542